Published by:
CBN Books
15 Winders Road
London
SW11 3HE
www.cookingbynumbers.com
Tel: 07979 812 234
Email: tom@cookingbynumbers.com

First published by CBN Books 2005
Text copyright © Tom Tuke-Hastings 2005
Photographs copyright © Tom Tuke-Hastings 2005

ISBN 0-9549698-0-4

Design and manufacture with thanks to:
Lee, Mike, Debbie, JK, Ed and Pete.

The right of Tom Tuke-Hastings as the author of the work has been asserted by him in accordance with the Copyright, Designs and Patents Act 1988.

A catalogue record for this book is available from the British Library.

All rights reserved. Without limiting the rights under copyright reserved above, no part of this publication may be reproduced, stored in or introduced into a retrieval system, or transmitted in any form by any means (electronic, mechanical, photocopying, recording, or otherwise) without prior written permission from the publisher.

Printed in Great Britain.

Legal cop out.
Alcohol can be dangerous to your health. None of these recipes are intended for those under the legal drinking age. The fantastic flavours may mask the alcohol content of the jellies. Please consume with moderation, don't drink and drive. If in doubt the vodka can be omitted. Quantities produced are approximate and there as a guide only.

Tom Tuke-Hastings

The Art of The VODKA JELLY

Life should NOT be a dull journey to the grave where you hope to arrive safely and in one piece. I aim to slide in sideways, champagne in hand, thoroughly worn out and screaming "AGAIN, AGAIN - what a sensational ride!"

This book is dedicated to my family and friends for making life so much fun.

Contents

Introduction	1
Tips on Jellies	2
Passion fruit	4
Vodka tonic	6
Raspberry	8
Cranberry	10
Rhubarb and custard	12
Mulled wine	14
Fresh orange	16
Caviar and lemon	18
Blackcurrant	20
Moscow mule	22
Cola	24
Peach	26
Coconut	28
Black grape	30
Elderflower fizz and raspberry	32
Bitter lemon	34
Russian coffee	36
Chilli	38
Champagne	40
Prawns	42
Pink grapefruit	44
Beetroot	46
Apricot	48
Bloody Mary	50

Introduction

This book has taken quite a while to write, not least due to the long and arduous testing process (extended by popular demand). Each jelly has been individually crafted and reworked to make the recipe you see before you. Many have fallen by the wayside and I am pleased to say, the nauseating taste and foul texture of the vodka and avocado jelly will never see the light of day again.

So why write a book on vodka jellies?

I have been mildly obsessed with vodka jellies for a long time. Every time I serve them, they make a huge impact. Whether it be a wild party or a civilised meal, they are a focal centrepiece and are always a lot of fun. They appeal to a huge range of age groups and I think everyone always enjoys the texture and theatre that is eating jelly.

I decided to refine the process of making vodka jellies. The traditional student method is to take a packet of jelly, melt it and mix it with too much cheap vodka. I decided that it could be much better and set out to turn the idea on its head, starting with a sensational cocktail of fresh fruit (and other) flavours, then working out how to set it. Not everything works, but that is the beauty of it, working within the natural restrictions and trying to find a suitable set.

I hope you enjoy the book and try the jellies.
Have fun!

Tom Tuke-Hastings

Tips on Jellies

I have tried to avoid using too much jargon in this book. The main culprit is the word 'sponge', explained below, along with a few hints and tips on jelly making.

All the recipes in this book use sachets as these are the easiest way to buy gelatine. These contain seven grams of gelatine powder. I have put all liquid measures in millilitres (ml) = 1/1000 of a litre.

Sponging gelatine: sponging is the process of taking the gelatine powder and turning it back into its true gelatinous form.

Put the liquid that you are using to sponge the gelatine into a heatproof bowl. Sprinkle the gelatine on top of this, so it covers the surface. Always pour the powder onto the liquid, never the other way around. If you are making a large batch, it is worth doing this in a big bowl, or even in smaller batches to ensure it all sponges correctly.

Leave the gelatine to absorb the liquid. It is ready once it has taken on a spongy, moist texture and becomes translucent. To melt this, place the bowl over gently simmering water. Stir the mixture as it gradually warms, until it becomes liquid.

Don't let the gelatine get too hot when melting it as this can ruin it. When mixing in the main ingredients, always mix them into the gelatine, not the other way around, as this can cause the gelatine to set in streaks, rather than combine to give a consistent set.

If you want to have pips etc suspended in a jelly, cool the finished mix by stirring it in a bowl over some iced water. Keep stirring until it reaches the consistency of thick custard. This will now hold the pips, rather than allowing them all to drop to the bottom.

Good luck!

Passion fruit

Passion fruit has always been one of my favourite fruits. Its intense flavours are matched by its visual splendour. The black pips stand in stark contrast to the yellow juice, giving a very smooth and flavour-filled jelly.

Ingredients:

12 passion fruit (150ml juice)
1/2 tablespoon sugar
50ml water
20ml vodka
1/2 sachet of gelatine
Makes 250ml

Method:

To juice the passion fruit, spoon out the pulp and seeds into a sieve. Using a spoon, push this around the sieve, until all the juice has passed into a bowl below. Put the juice with half the pips, the sugar, water and vodka. Sprinkle the gelatine over two tablespoons of water and sponge. Melt it over simmering water and stir in the mixture.

I like to have the seeds floating through the jelly. To do this, put the mixture in a bowl over iced water and keep stirring as it cools. When the mixture becomes thick it can be poured and set, allowing the pips to be suspended.

Vodka tonic

Another of the classic cocktail incarnations of vodka. This is a tasty jelly, but is most notable for its appearance. The fizzy tonic gives off large bubbles which are captured in the jelly as it sets, giving a sensational visual effect.

Ingredients:

400ml tonic
1 lemon
40ml vodka
1 sachet of gelatine
Makes 450ml

Method:

Sponge the gelatine in three tablespoons of water. Juice the lemon and combine it with the vodka and tonic.

Melt the gelatine over some simmering water. Pour the tonic mixture into this and combine. Decant this into your vessels and set.

This is a very clear jelly and I sometimes like to set slices of lemon into it to give it some more colour. However, it still looks great on its own, showcasing the bubbles.

Raspberry

Raspberries are one of my favourite fruits and this jelly is packed full of their explosive flavour. Their deep red is magnificent, but even better is the flavour, which is balanced by the sweet chocolate.

Ingredients:

300g fresh raspberries
50ml cranberry juice
1 tablespoon sugar
35ml vodka
1/2 packet of gelatine
Chocolate to decorate
Makes 450ml

Method:

Sponge the gelatine in three tablespoons of water. Liquidise the raspberries (you need 250ml) and sieve to remove the pips. Combine the cranberry juice with the remaining pulp and pass through the sieve again.

Place the raspberry puree and cranberry juice together. Add the sugar and vodka then stir until the sugar has dissolved. Melt the gelatine and combine the two mixtures. I like to decorate this with spikes of chocolate, but you can melt it, put spirals on top, shave it, shape it, or whatever you feel like.

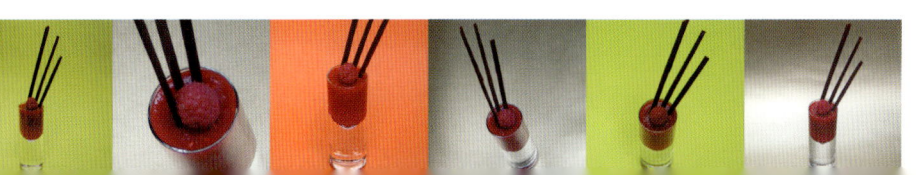

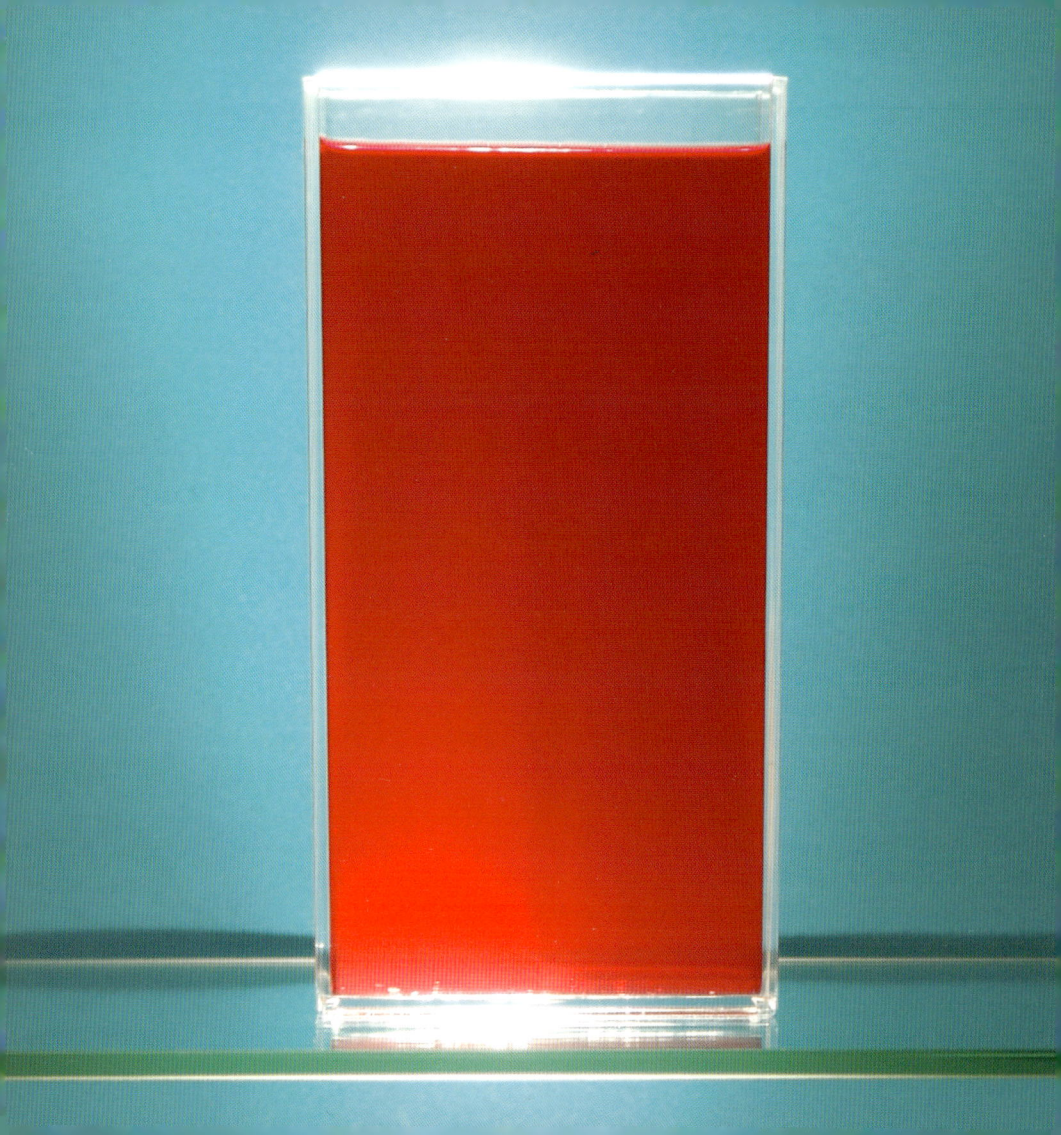

Cranberry

Vodka cranberry is a favourite in bars across the world. The tart juice combines well with the spirits, to give a fabulous blend. This is a very quick jelly to make and it tastes great, so give it a go.

Ingredients:

800ml cranberry juice
100ml vodka
1 lemon
2 sachets of gelatine
Makes 1100ml

Method:

Juice the lemon and strain off the pips, then mix it in with the cranberry juice and vodka.

Sprinkle the gelatine on eight additional tablespoons of cranberry juice. Allow it to sponge and melt it over a saucepan on simmering water. Add the cranberry mixture into this and decant for setting.

This is a beautifully clear jelly and it looks great en masse. Try putting it in vases or other large glass containers. The jelly will of course take any shape, so have fun!

Rhubarb and custard

This might sound a little strange and not what you would expect to have as a jelly. But it is something special. The colour is magnificent and the flavour spot on. Rhubarb and custard is great hot, but even better as a vodka jelly.

Ingredients:

450g rhubarb (as thin and red as possible)
200ml water
3 tablespoons castor sugar
50ml vodka
1 sachet of gelatine
Thick custard
Makes 550ml

Method:

Finely slice the rhubarb and place it in a pan with the water and sugar. Bring it to the boil and simmer until cooked. Leave this on the side to cool. Make some nice thick custard (you only need about half a pint). Once cooked, allow to cool.

Sponge the gelatine in four tablespoons of water and allow to melt. Stir the rhubarb and vodka into this. The mixture can now be decanted into glasses. Leave a little space on top and once the jelly has set, pour on a layer of the custard.

Mulled wine

Mulled wine is usually considered for the festive season only and you normally expect it to come piping hot. Try it cold as a great jelly.

Ingredients:

750ml red wine
500ml orange juice
75g castor sugar
1/2 teaspoon mixed spice
1/2 teaspoon cinnamon
125ml vodka
2 1/2 sachets of gelatine
Makes 1,500ml

Method:

Mix the wine and orange juice together. Sponge the gelatine in 125ml of this mixture. Then melt it over simmering water. Stir the orange and wine into this and combine. Add the spices and vodka to the main mixture and stir well. Pour into glasses to set.

It is worth allowing this mixture to cool a little before pouring it into vessels. This will allow the spices to be integrated the whole way through the jelly, as they can settle to the bottom.

Fresh orange

Vodka has been partnered with orange for years and for good reasons. Break away from the image of it as breakfast drink, or a dreadful sixties starter and drag it into the 21st century in a new format.

Ingredients:

8 oranges (650ml juice)
65ml vodka
1 1/2 sachets of gelatine
Makes 720ml

Method:

Squeeze the oranges and strain the juice. Use additional oranges if you need more juice. You can use juice from a carton, it won't taste as nice, but the colour will be stronger.

Sponge the gelatine in six tablespoons of the juice. Once it has sponged, heat it over a saucepan of simmering water until it melts.

Mix the rest of the juice into the gelatine until it is fully mixed in.

Add the vodka, stir it in well and pour into containers. Set and serve. Try making this with blood oranges for a richer pink colour.

Caviar and lemon

Caviar is often served with vodka and what could sum up Russian luxury better? This is naturally a more savoury jelly that can be served as a starter, an intermediate course or even as an hors-d'oeuvre.

Ingredients:

55g tin of caviar or herrings roe
Juice of 2 lemons
800ml water
100ml vodka
2 sachets of gelatine
Makes 1,000ml

Method:

Sponge the gelatine in six tablespoons of water and then melt over some simmering water. Into this mix the water and lemon juice. Once it is well mixed in, add the vodka.

Allow this to cool for a while until it takes on the consistency of custard. You can speed this up by stirring the liquid in a bowl over some iced water.

Once it has thickened, add the caviar and gently stir it in so that it is equally distributed. Then decant and finish the refrigeration process.

Blackcurrant

Blackcurrants have a vivid colour and an intense flavour. I have added cream to this recipe which brings out the colour, without taking anything away from the full-bodied flavour.

Ingredients:

680g jar of blackcurrants in syrup
150ml cream
70ml vodka
2 sachets of gelatine
Makes 750ml

Method:

Drain half of the juice off the berries and put to one side. Put the rest of the juice and the berries in a blender (retaining some berries for decoration). Blend until they form a smooth mixture.

Stir in the cream and vodka.

Sponge the gelatine in eight tablespoons of the leftover juice, using water if you don't have enough.

Pour into containers and decorate with the reserved berries.

Moscow mule

This jelly harnesses the refreshing and fiery edge of ginger. It tingles on the tongue, giving a sensational clean and fresh taste. This is quick, easy and very popular, so give it a go.

Ingredients:

800ml ginger beer
Juice of 3 lemons
100ml vodka
2 sachets of gelatine
Makes 950ml

Method:

Juice the lemons, strain the pips and bits out and then mix the juice into the ginger beer. Sponge the gelatine in eight tablespoons of the mixture.

Melt the sponged gelatine over some simmering water. Mix the vodka in the remainder of the mixture. Then combine this into the molten gelatine, pour into glasses and set.

This is a dynamic jelly and the bubbles look fantastic. Try setting it in tall vases to create a dramatic centrepiece.

Cola

Vodka and cola is a tried and tested mix. The flavour is a given, known to people all around the world. As a jelly, it retains the colour and bubbles. An icon of capitalism, with a shot of communism's favourite tipple secreted inside.

Ingredients:

660ml of cola
1 lemon
70ml of vodka
2 sachets of gelatine
Makes 800ml

Method:

This is a very quick and easy recipe that is ready in no time.

Sponge the gelatine in eight tablespoons of water. Once it has sponged, melt it over some simmering water.

Pour in the cola and vodka and mix together. Juice the lemon, strain it to remove the pips and bits then put with the cola. Combine this mix into the molten gelatine.

Pour into glasses and set. I have served this here with a slice of lemon to mimic the normal serving suggestion.

Peach

This recipe can be used with either peaches or nectarines. Both give an excellent colour, fabulous taste and even smell great as well.

Ingredients:

8 peaches
50ml orange juice
80ml vodka
1 1/2 sachets of gelatine
Makes 900ml

Method:

Take the peaches and simmer them in the orange juice. Once they have cooked down and collapsed, remove the stones and skins.

When they have cooled down, liquidise them. You should have about 700ml of juice, if not, top it up with orange juice.

Sponge the gelatine in six tablespoons of water and then melt.

Add the vodka to the juice and mix it into the gelatine. Pour into vessels and set.

Coconut

This is a rich and strong jelly, brimming to the top with the tropical flavour of coconut. The colour is (not surprisingly) as white as milk, giving a striking effect, especially when it is partnered against strong colourful backgrounds.

Ingredients:

One 400ml tin of coconut milk
100ml water
1 tablespoon sugar
50ml vodka
1 sachet of gelatine
Makes 550ml

Method:

Sponge the gelatine in four tablespoons of water. Combine the coconut milk with the water and sugar and mix well until all the sugar has dissolved.

Add the vodka to the coconut and mix into the gelatine. Pour into containers and serve.

If making a large quantity, you can set it in coconut shells with the tops cut off. To get these to set in the fridge, put the coconut shells in a wide-necked glass so it can be positioned upright while setting.

Black grape

Grapes and alcohol are synonymous. Wine has been made for thousands of years, but the juice on its own has its own distinct and pleasant taste. Partnered with a little vodka, this makes a colourful and sumptuous union.

Ingredients:

1 litre black grape juice
100ml vodka
2 sachets of gelatine
Makes 1,100ml

Method:

Take eight tablespoons of the grape juice and sponge the gelatine in this.

Once it has sponged, melt it over some simmering water. Put the remainder of the juice and vodka together and stir slowly into the molten gelatine.

Pour this into containers and set. Due to the dark colour and excellent transparency, this looks great in tall thin containers, just make sure you have a long enough spoon to get those bits out of the bottom.

Elderflower fizz and raspberry

This is another favourite jelly. It is a cinch to make, but looks and tastes great. The suspended raspberries look fantastic and there is something about it that always reminds me of summer.

Ingredients:

900ml fizzy elderflower drink
2 punnets of raspberries (dependent on serving)
80ml vodka
2 sachets of gelatine
Make 1,000ml

Method:

Sponge the gelatine in six tablespoons of elderflower fizz. Once it has sponged, melt it over some simmering water. Combine the remainder of the fizz with the vodka and mix it into the gelatine.

Pour it into containers, leaving some space at the top and drop a raspberry in. You may need to push it into the mix until the whole berry is under the jelly. If you are making a big bowl, you can cover the entire surface with the berries, or mix them up. They also look good as a layer in the middle. To do this, half fill the bowl with jelly, covering the surface with berries, then set it. Once it is set, you can pour on another layer of jelly and more berries.

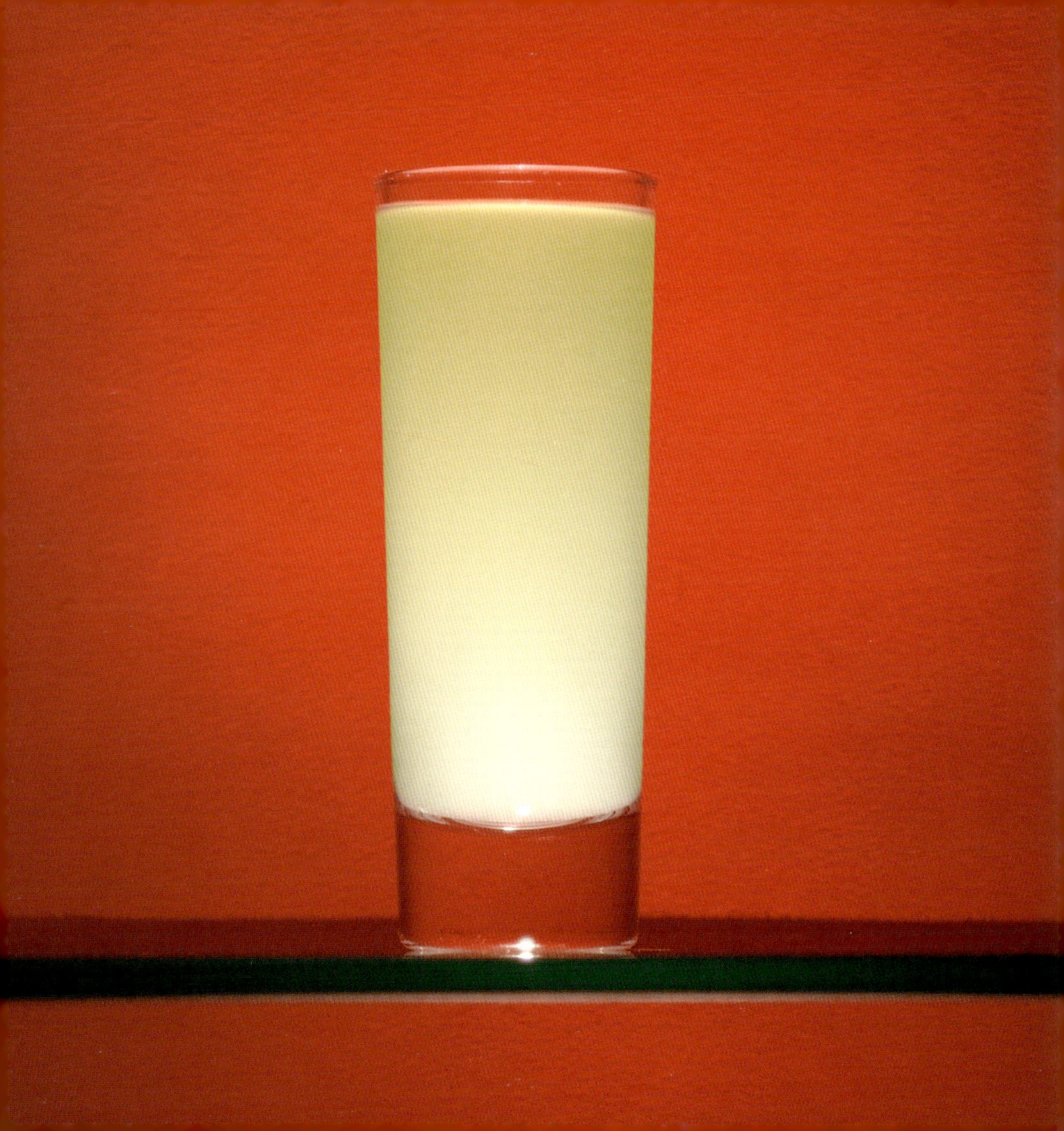

Bitter lemon

This is another great easy jelly. The set is firm and clear. The bitter lemon is given an extra kick from the fresh lemon juice, that really hits home. Give it a go as a crisp jelly to cleanse the palate.

Ingredients:

800ml bitter lemon
2 lemons
100ml vodka
2 sachets of gelatine
Makes 1,000ml

Method:

Sponge the gelatine in six tablespoons of water. Once it is ready, melt it over some simmering water.

Combine the bitter lemon, lemon juice and vodka and mix it into the molten jelly. Pour into glasses and set.

That's it, it's that quick and easy, so no excuses for not giving it a try.

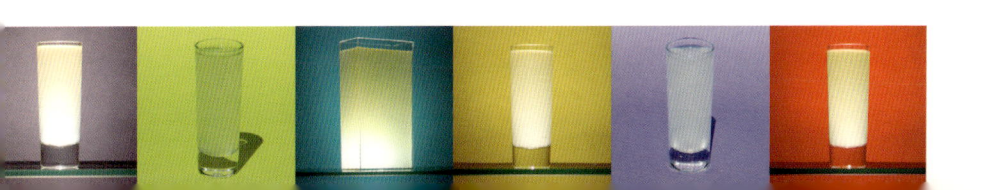

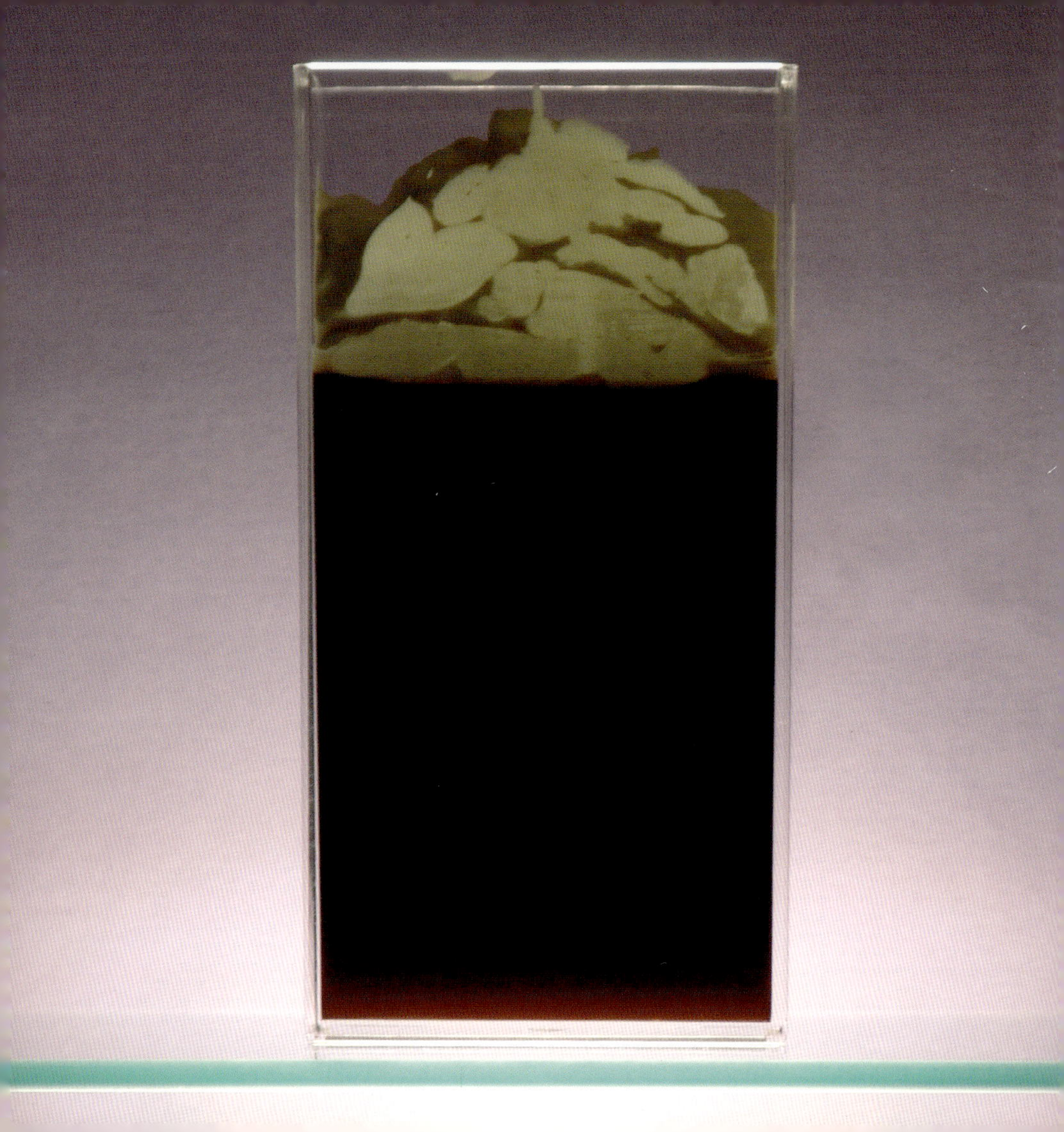

Russian coffee

Russian coffee mixes strong aromatic coffee with vodka and smooth whipped cream. The strength of the coffee is enhanced by the flavour of the vodka and the voluptuous smoothness of the cream.

Ingredients:

400ml strong coffee
2 tablespoons sugar
45ml vodka
1 sachet of gelatine
Whipped cream to serve
Makes 450ml

Method:

Sponge the gelatine in four tablespoons of water.

Make the coffee and once the gelatine has sponged, add this slowly, stirring all the time. If necessary, heat this gently so all the gelatine melts.

Allow this to cool to room temperature and add the vodka.

Pour into glasses and set in the fridge. When ready to serve, whip the cream and put a good dollop on top of all the servings.

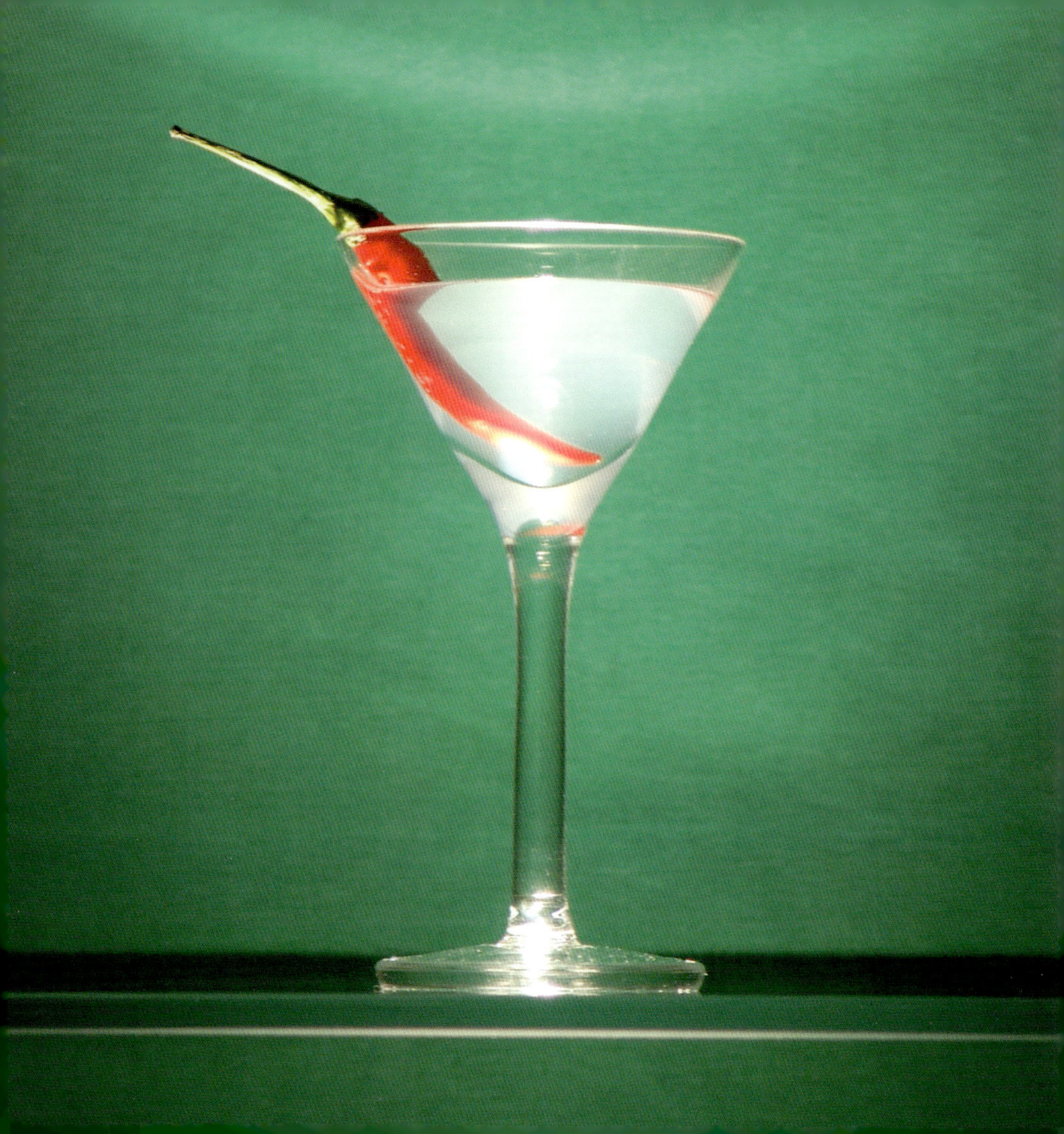

Chilli

Latin fire spreads through the very heart of this jelly. Hot and spicy, it excites the mouth and tingles on the tongue. Try experimenting with different chillies, but beware, these can be pretty hot.

Ingredients:

1 chilli
300ml water
30ml vodka
1 red chilli
1 sachet of gelatine
Makes 350ml

Method:

Finely dice the chilli and mix it with the water and vodka. Sprinkle the gelatine over four tablespoons of water. Once the gelatine has sponged, melt it over a saucepan of simmering water.

Strain the chilli mix and slowly stir it into the melted gelatine until it is a smooth consistency. Then pour into containers.

This is a clear jelly, so I like to make it more colourful by setting a whole chilli in it. Though you might want to leave these on the side when it comes to eating.

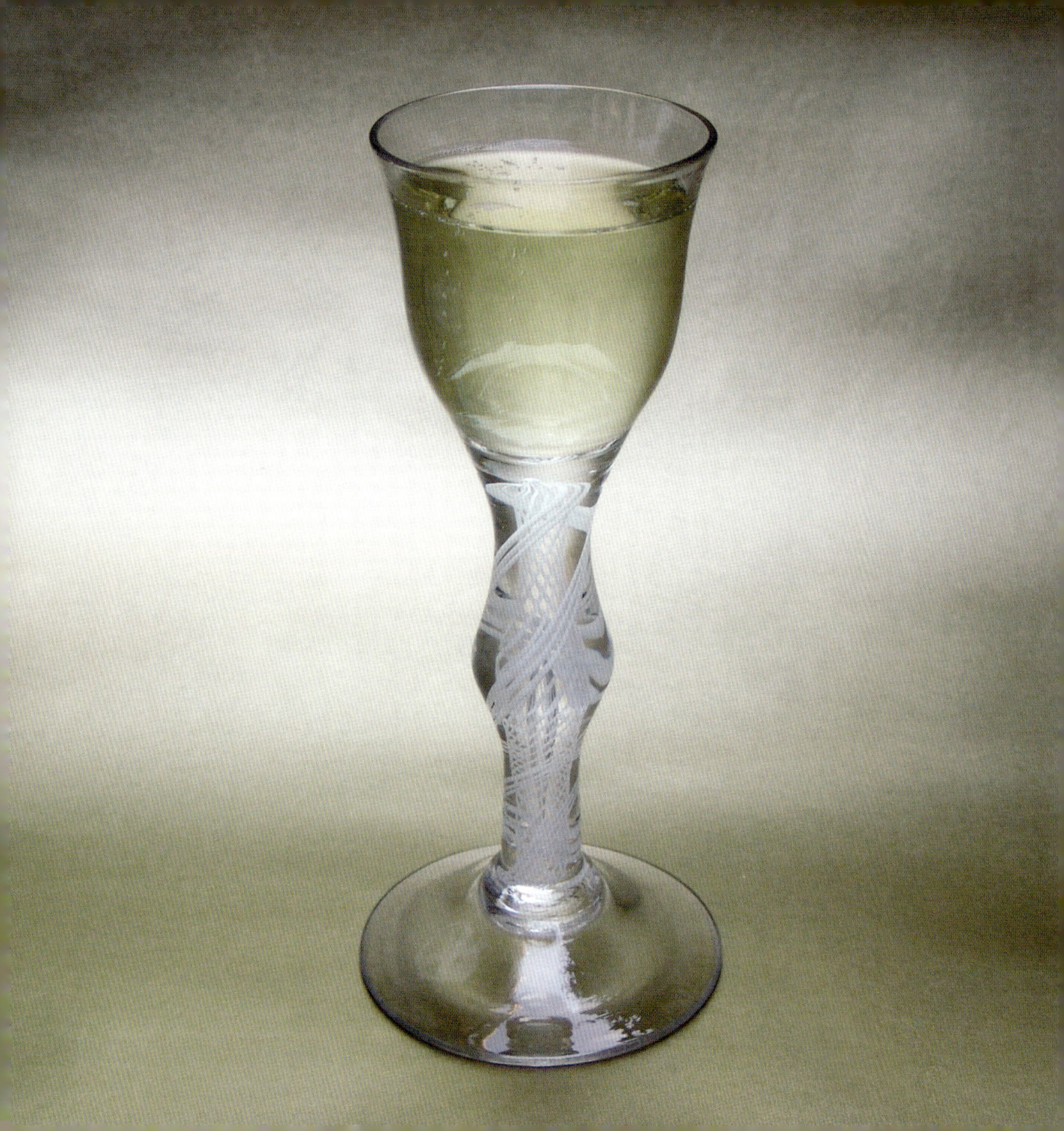

Champagne

Champagne is considered the king of wines. Partner it with the king of spirits and you have a great combination. I use less vodka in this to allow the subtle flavours of the champagne to show through.

Ingredients:

1 bottle of champagne
2 tablespoons of sugar
50ml vodka
2 sachets of gelatine
Makes 800ml

Method:

Sponge the gelatine in eight tablespoons of water. Once it is ready, melt it over some simmering water. Mix the vodka and sugar into the gelatine.

Once the sugar has dissolved, add the champagne and stir until it is mixed in. Avoid overstirring as this will knock the bubbles out. I like to use cold champagne as this keeps more of the bubbles.

Decant and chill. If using champagne flutes, it is worth setting the fridge up to take them before you decant them, to avoid the glasses not fitting in.

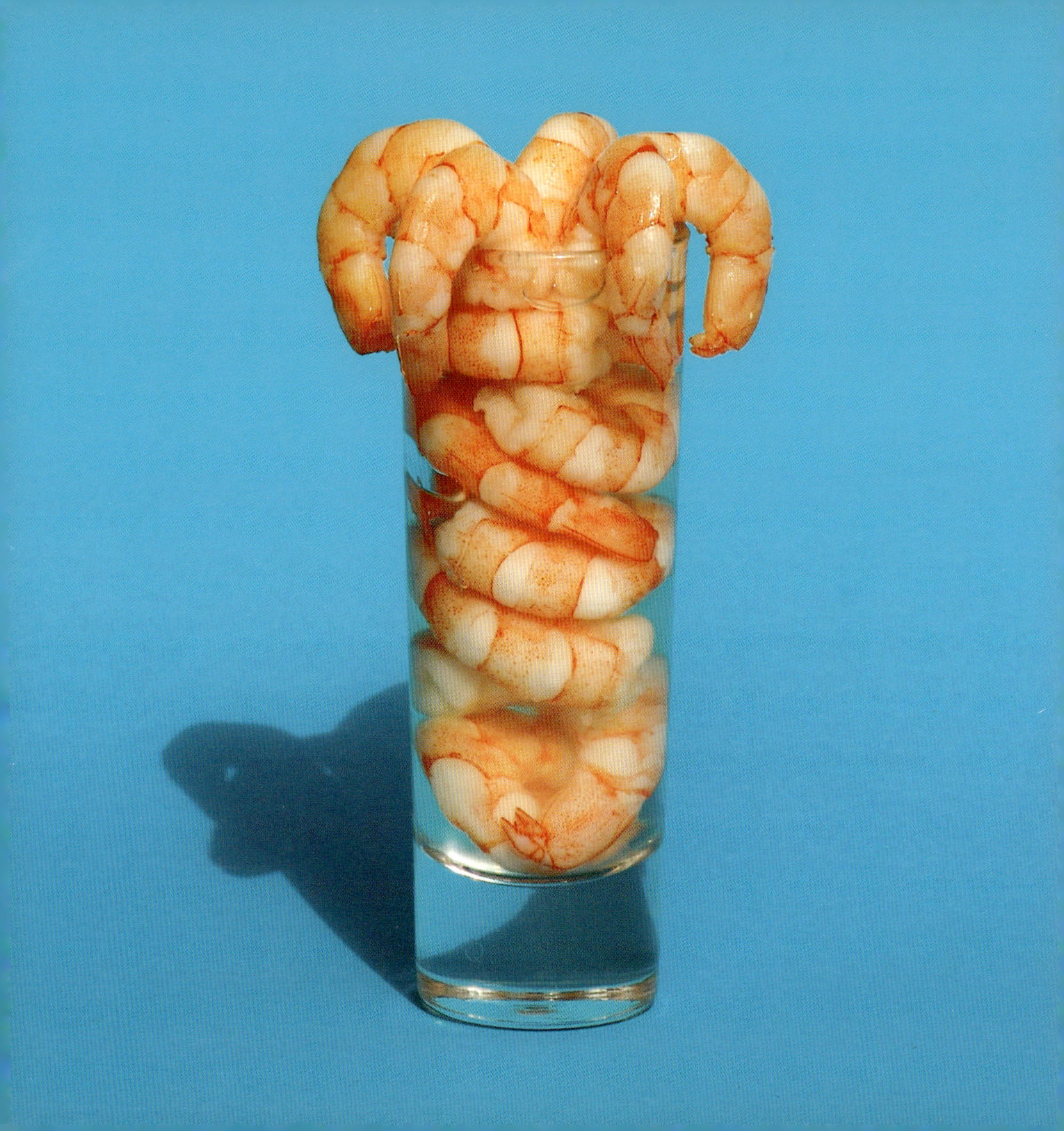

Prawns

Bright, pink and slightly unexpected, these add a splash of colour and finesse to any table. They are a more savoury option, but a fun and exciting one.

Ingredients:

110g fresh prawns
Juice of 2 lemons
900ml water
100ml vodka
2 sachets of gelatine
Makes 1,100ml

Method:

Sponge the gelatine in six tablespoons of water. Once it is ready, melt it over some simmering water.

Mix in the lemon juice, water and vodka.

Decant this into containers, decorate with the prawns and set.

When storing this in the fridge, I recommend covering it with cling film to keep the prawns moist.

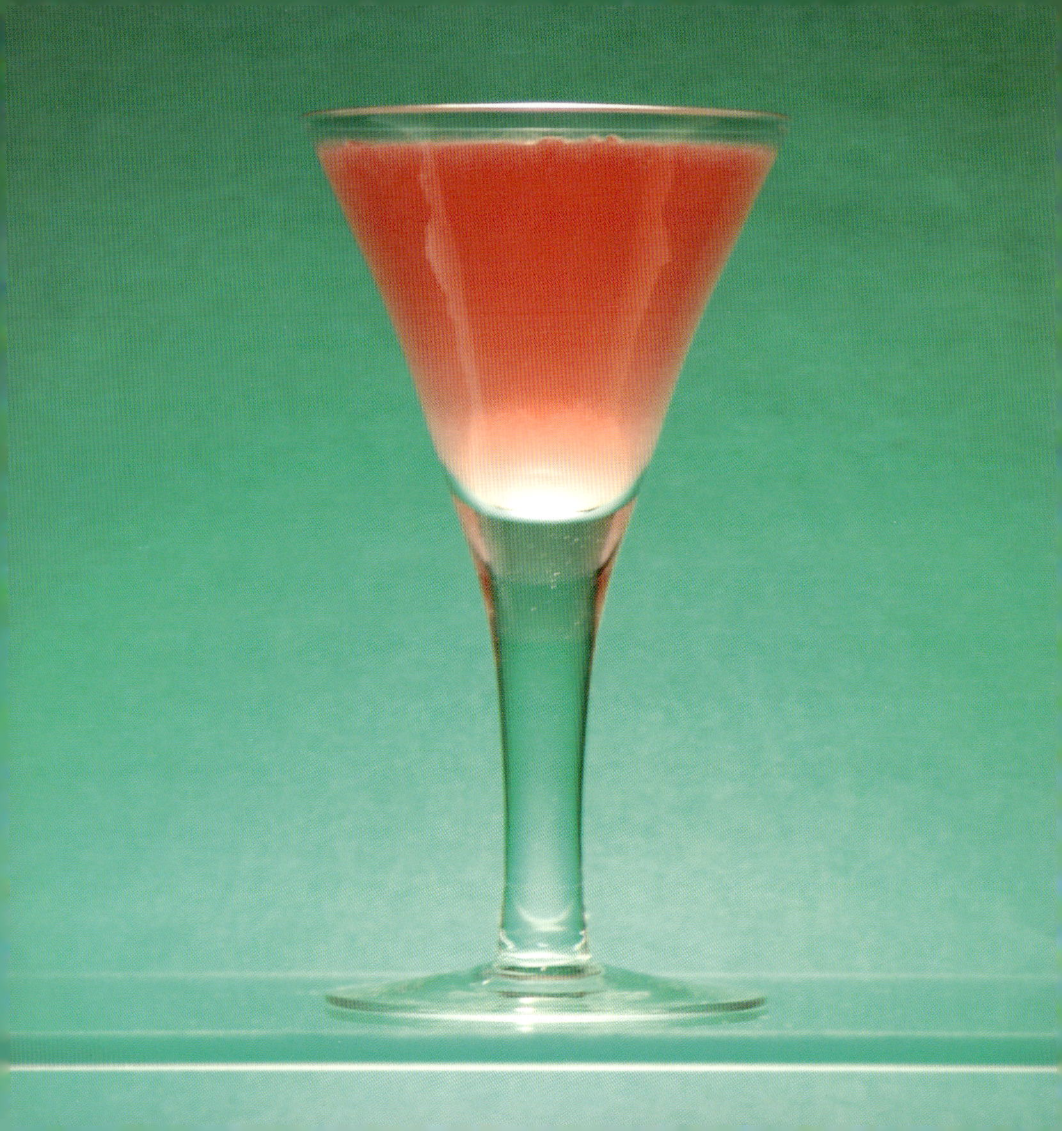

Pink grapefruit

Smooth, luscious and tart, the grapefruit is a jewel inside its rugged skin. The pink variety has the added benefit of its majestic colour. This brightens up the jelly and makes you forsake the plain variety.

Ingredients:

2 pink grapefruits
1 tablespoon sugar
50ml vodka
1 sachet of gelatine
Makes 450ml

Method:

Sponge the gelatine in four tablespoons of water.

Juice and strain the grapefruits (you need 400ml of juice). Add the sugar and vodka and mix until the sugar dissolves.

Melt the gelatine and stir in the juice mixture.

Pour into receptacles and set.

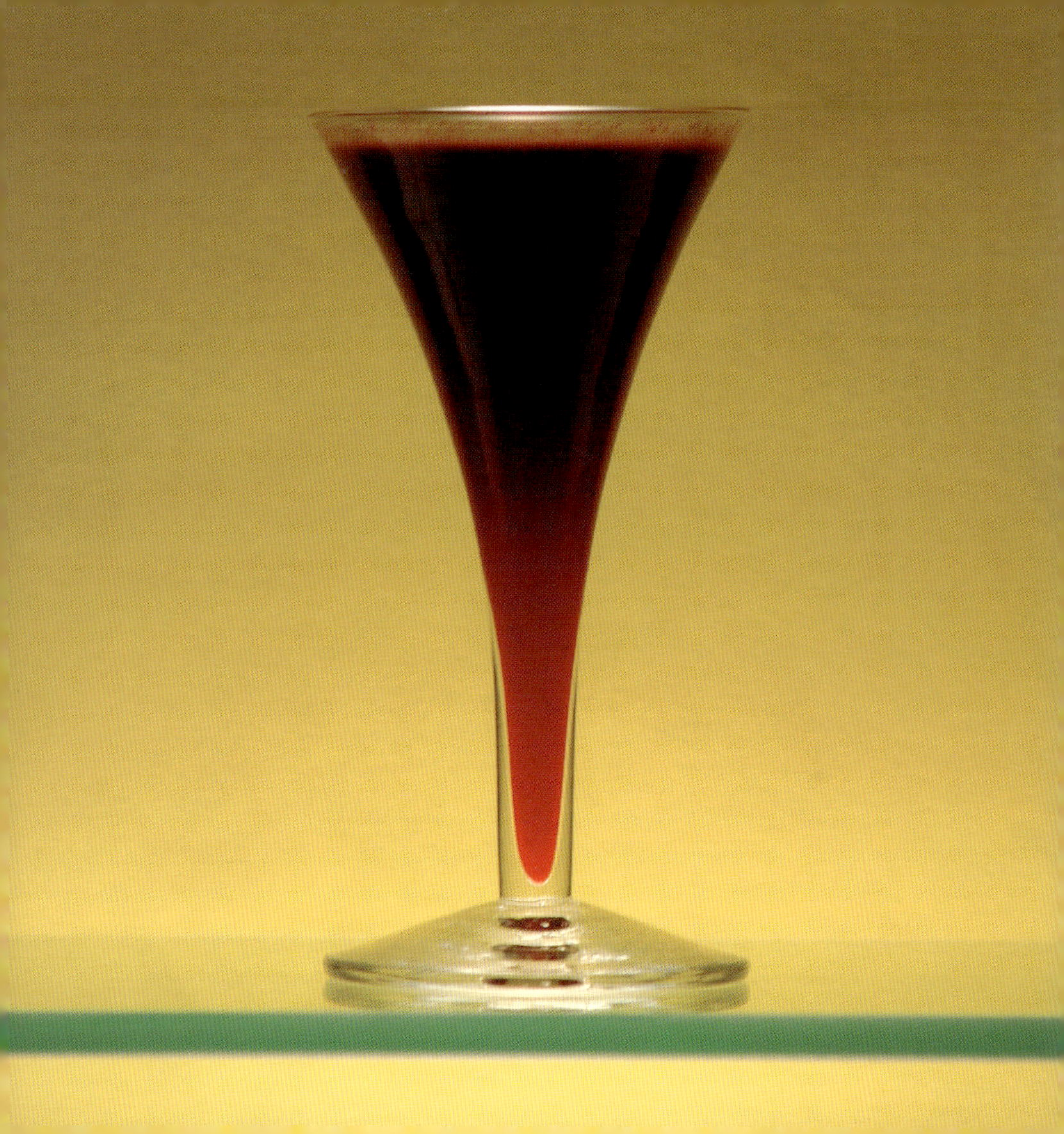

Beetroot

Bortsch, the famous Russian beetroot soup, is powerful and deep in colour. This is mirrored here with this very deep red jelly. The vodka gives the beetroot an additional complexity which works well.

Ingredients:

250g of cooked beetroot
50ml vodka
1 teaspoon ground pepper
1 1/2 sachets of gelatine
Makes 550ml

Method:

Sponge the gelatine in six tablespoons of water.

Roughly chop the beetroot and put it in a blender with 200ml of water. Liquefy the mixture and strain to remove any lumps. Blend the lumps again and pass through a sieve until all of it is liquefied.

Add the vodka and pepper. Melt the gelatine and mix in the beetroot and vodka.

Pour the liquid into containers and set. Be careful not to spill any as the beetroot stains like nothing on earth.

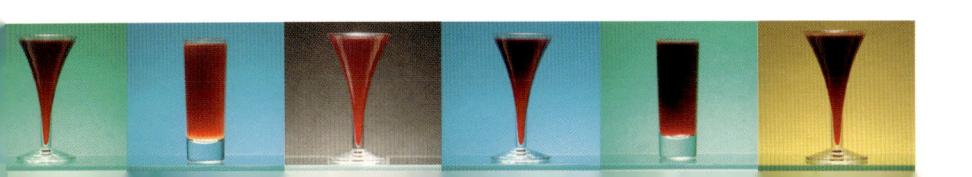

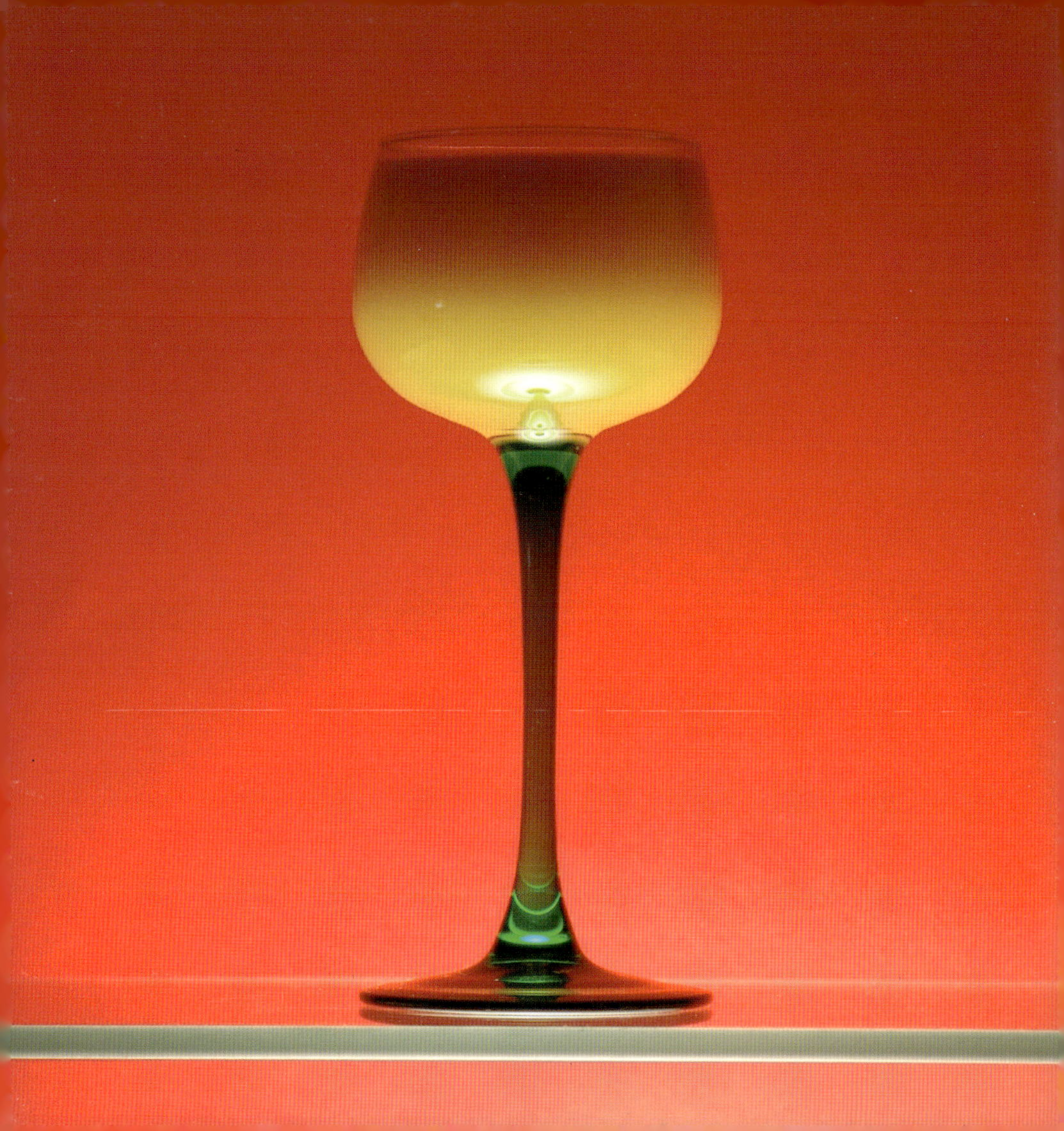

Apricot

Smooth and tangy, the apricot changes its texture when made into a jelly. The soft furry skin is gone, but the sumptuous softness of the texture more than makes up for it. The colour is retained and a fine jelly is born.

Ingredients:

550g fresh apricots (stoned)
400ml orange juice
6 tablespoons sugar
75ml vodka
2 sachets of gelatine
Makes 850ml

Method:

Roughly chop the apricots and place in a saucepan. Gently simmer with half the juice and the sugar.

Once the apricots have broken down, liquefy them and strain to remove any lumps. Liquefy the lumps and strain again until it is all liquid. Top up with the rest of the orange juice until you have 750ml of juice.

Sponge the gelatine in eight tablespoons of orange juice, then melt over some simmering water. Add the vodka to the apricot and mix it into the gelatine. Pour and set.

Bloody Mary

Hot and tangy, this well-known hangover cure takes well to being a jelly. It has a strong and majestic red colour that blazes away, and a firm texture for a more filling jelly.

Ingredients:

1 litre tomato juice
3 tablespoons Lea and Perrins Worcester sauce
3 teaspoons chilli sauce
Juice of 2 lemons
A good pinch of salt and pepper
150ml vodka
1 3/4 sachets of gelatine
Makes 1,250ml

Method:

Sponge the gelatine in eight tablespoons of water.

Mix the remainder of the ingredients together. You might want to start with less chilli and then add it to taste, as this is a hot jelly.

Melt the gelatine and combine the mixture into this. Pour and set.

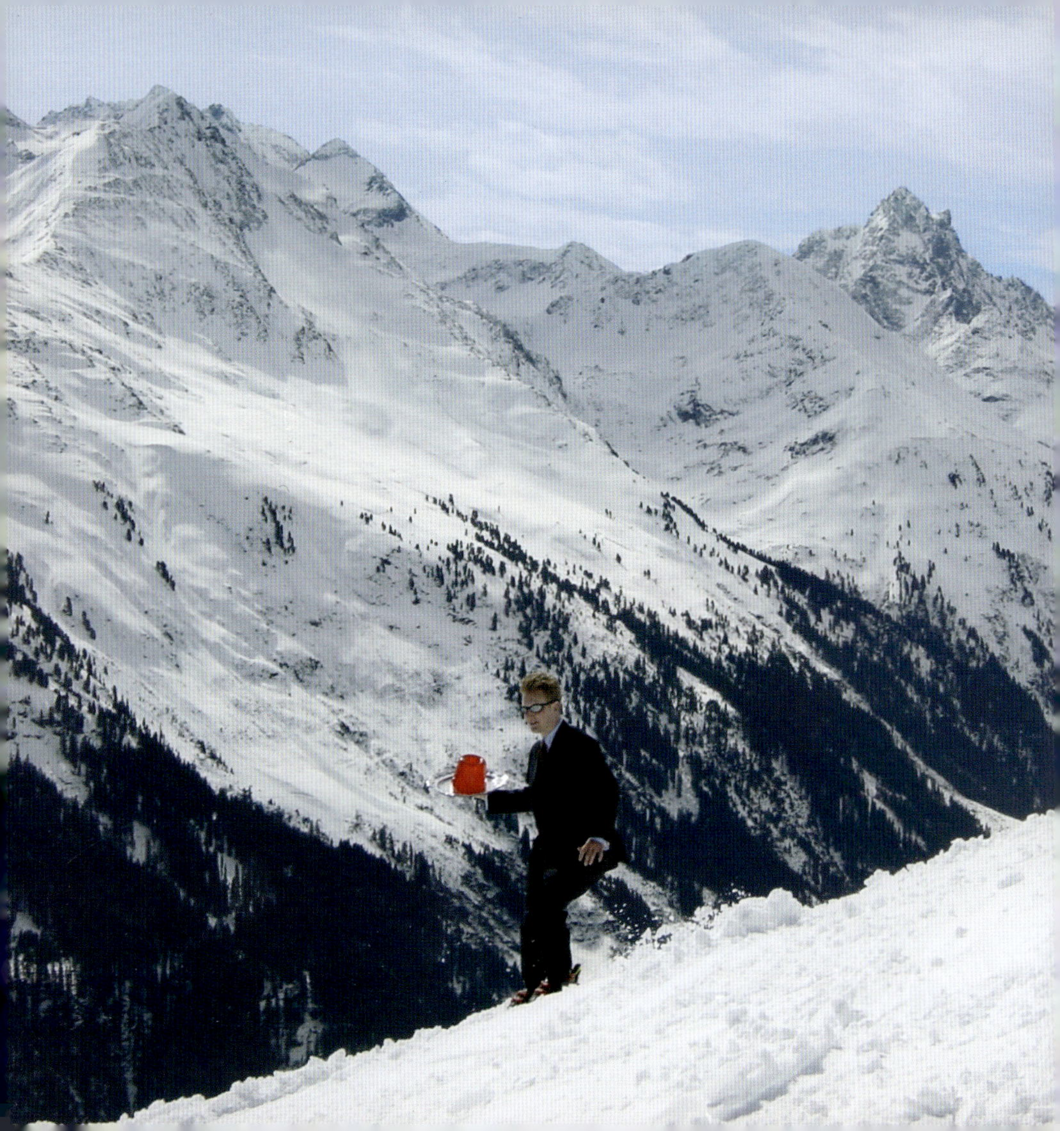